TRAINS ON THE MIDLAND MAIN LINE

John Jackson

AMBERLEY

First published 2019

Amberley Publishing
The Hill, Stroud
Gloucestershire, GL5 4EP

www.amberley-books.com

Copyright © John Jackson, 2019

The right of John Jackson to be identified as
the Author of this work has been asserted in
accordance with the Copyrights, Designs and
Patents Act 1988.

ISBN 978 1 4456 7600 5 (print)
ISBN 978 1 4456 7601 2 (ebook)

British Library Cataloguing in Publication Data.
A catalogue record for this book is available from
the British Library.

Origination by Amberley Publishing.
Printed in the UK.

Introduction

As a regular traveller along the length of the Midland Main Line (MML) between London and Sheffield, I often reflect on what might have been. The ongoing erection of electrification masts between Bedford, Kettering and Corby reminds me of a remarkable change of fortunes on the MML. In the 1960s, the line was considered to be no more than an unnecessary duplication of railway tracks heading north from the capital.

Only history will record just how close this line came to being closed completely under the notorious Beeching Axe. That axe fell swiftly after his reports on the future direction of the UK's railways were published in the 1960s. The widespread closure of railway stations and passenger lines that was to follow might well have included stretches of the Midland Main Line.

In particular, the section between Bedford and Leicester was identified as a strong candidate for complete closure. The spur from Kettering to Corby was one such victim, with passenger services being withdrawn in 1966.

Today, Corby is not only back on the railway map but is soon to be the northern terminus of electric services from London St Pancras. Lengthy stretches of railway tracks on the main line itself that were deemed superfluous and lifted are being replaced so the southern end of the MML can once again become a four-track railway.

In this book we take a journey northward on the Midland Main Line from London's imposing St Pancras station to the route's principal terminus in the Yorkshire city of Sheffield. It is a journey that takes in the cities of Leicester, Derby and Nottingham. It offers scenery ranging from the landscape legacy of industrial cities to the open spaces of the Derbyshire Dales, and much more in between.

The line between London and Bedford was electrified in the early 1980s. Since then, the services on this section of the MML have evolved into a north to south cross-London service that now offers through running to Gatwick Airport and Brighton. These services ordinarily use the reopened Snow Hill tunnel, with St Pancras International's low-level platforms opening in 2007 to replace King's Cross Thameslink on the nearby Pentonville Road. The services between Bedford and Brighton, with other destinations served south of the Thames, are in the hands of Govia Thameslink Railway. Govia is a joint enterprise between the Go Ahead Group and French-based Keolis.

The train shed at St Pancras is also shared by Eurostar, offering services through the Channel Tunnel to mainland Europe, together with domestic operator Southeastern, operating trains to the Kent coast. Both these operators use the High Speed 1 rail line. These tracks diverge from the MML shortly after the St Pancras platform ends and head eastwards towards Stratford International.

Most passenger trains operate between London and Sheffield via Derby station with a few peak trains travelling via Nottingham, where reversal is necessary to reach Chesterfield and Sheffield, via Ilkeston. Nottingham station also lies at the centre of an important cross-country route that links Liverpool and Manchester in the North West with Peterborough, Ely and Norwich in East Anglia. These services are routed via Sheffield, where the trains reverse, and traverse the Midland Main Line south from there in order to reach Nottingham.

Our journey through these pages is one that follows today's route from London's split-level station at St Pancras. It is a journey reflecting the line in the twenty-first century. By way of comparison, we also take a look at a variety of trains to be seen on the line around the time of rail privatisation, approaching a quarter of a century ago.

The rail journey from London to Sheffield (via Derby) is an end to end passenger journey that takes just under two hours, giving it a competitive chance against alternative transport competitors. Today, these longer distance services are in the hands of the current franchise holder, East Midlands Trains (EMT), owned by the Stagecoach Group. The company's main line rolling stock is provided by a fleet of four, five and seven-coach Meridian Class 222 diesel units, introduced from 2003, contrasting with a fleet of High Speed Train (HST) Class 43 power cars and coaching stock dating back to the 1970s. These HSTs have been a familiar sight on the Midland Main Line since the early 1980s.

In its very early nineteenth-century days, the Midland Railway relied upon Rugby as the interchange between its own services within the East Midlands and those of the London & Birmingham Railway via the West Coast Main Line into London's Euston station.

In order to reduce the congestion caused at Rugby, an alternative route south was constructed later in the nineteenth century which linked Leicester with London, providing access via an interchange at Hitchin. This route is maintained today, running through Kettering, Wellingborough and as far as Bedford. The new route simply moved the capacity bottleneck from Rugby to Hitchin. The Midland Railway's solution was to reach the capital by way of a newly constructed line from Bedford via Luton.

This new route south from Leicester to London totals approximately 99 miles, with today's fastest non-stop journey time of just sixty-five minutes.

For much of the route north of Leicester, the London to Nottingham, Derby and Sheffield trains pass through the very heart of what I recall from my schoolboy geography days was described as 'The Yorks, Notts and Derby coalfield'. The continuous movement of coal was a feature of MML freight traffic, particularly on the northern half of its route, until that industry's demise. Instead, today's freight trains on the line are more likely to contain materials for the UK construction sector.

In the pages that follow, we also look at the cross section of non-passenger trains that use this line today. This includes a glimpse at the Loughborough works of Brush Engineering, a company whose history is synonymous with the rail industry.

We also include a look at the area around Toton, on the border between Derbyshire and Nottinghamshire. The yard, and the depot of the same name, nestles at the southern end of the Erewash Valley Line, which bisects the passenger routes via Derby and Nottingham.

Today, Toton depot is the maintenance hub for DB Cargo's locomotive fleet. The area's freight yards have declined in importance as the demand for domestic coal has fallen sharply. The yards are still, however, visited by various operators' locos, a number of examples of which are featured here.

One of the more controversial railway line closures in the aftermath of the Beeching proposals saw the through route between London St Pancras and Manchester via Miller's Dale, in the Derbyshire Peak District, closed completely to the north of Matlock. This closure consigned named express trains such as The Palatine and the Blue Pullman to history. Today, for MML users, Manchester is reached via a change of train at Sheffield, and a service westbound along Derbyshire's Hope Valley route. An EMT-operated diesel multiple unit service, between Derby and Matlock, is all that remains of this truncated route today.

In the mid-twentieth century, between rail nationalisation and subsequent privatisation, MML passengers travelling to the north were offered through services to the north of Sheffield with workings to Scotland, via Leeds and the Settle and Carlisle line. These included named trains such as The Thames–Clyde Express which, as the name implies, linked London with Glasgow via the MML. Edinburgh was similarly served by The Waverley.

Today, services to the north of Sheffield are limited to a few HST through workings to and from Wakefield Westgate and Leeds in the early morning and late evening. The latter city's Neville Hill depot services the HST fleet on behalf of East Midlands Trains, making these through workings operationally convenient. A further variation of this northern route saw a working through to York and, in the summer months, Scarborough.

As I write this introduction, future electrification plans would appear to have been scaled back and will now be confined to an extension from Bedford to Corby, leaving the MML at Kettering North Junction, with diesel power remaining for the time being north of here. There is even a suggestion that future traction might be a bi-mode operation, with the units involved switching from electric to diesel at this point.

Further, HS2 will have a geographical impact on the MML route map, particularly from the Toton area northwards to Sheffield – subject, of course, to the line actually being built!

Meanwhile, putting future speculation to one side, I hope you enjoy your journey through the pages that follow as much as I have enjoyed compiling them.

John Jackson

This Midland Main Line (MML) route map shows the principal stations served on the route from London St Pancras to Sheffield. In the East Midlands the line splits to serve Derby and Nottingham before joining again south of Chesterfield. A limited service also operates north of Sheffield, serving Leeds, York and Scarborough. On the pages that follow, we trace the route of the MML northwards from St Pancras to Sheffield. We also take a look back at the route a quarter of a century ago, in the decade of rail privatisation.

Our Midland Main Line journey begins at London's St Pancras station. East Midlands Trains continues to use four of the platforms on the ground level at the station, which dates back to 1868. These services are in the hands of Class 222 Meridians, introduced from 2003 onwards, and High Speed Trains (HSTs) which date back to the 1970s. On 2 September 2017, No. 222015 *175 Years of Derby Railways 1839 – 2014* stands alongside HST power car No. 43045 in the terminus at St Pancras.

Today, these HSTs are primarily used on an hourly service to Nottingham, usually with Market Harborough as the first call after leaving London. On 20 May 2017, No. 43058 is seen on the rear of a Nottingham-bound service.

In the mornings and evenings, HSTs also operate on services to and from Leeds. This is primarily for operational purposes as these sets are maintained at that city's Neville Hill depot. On 27 April 2017, No. 43043 has just terminated on a morning service from Leeds.

The faster services to Sheffield, operated hourly via Leicester and Derby, are in the hands of seven-car Meridians. On the same day, No. 222003 *Tornado* waits to form the next departure to Sheffield. These flagship services cover the distance of around 140 miles in a journey time of just under two hours, usually calling only at Leicester, Derby and Chesterfield.

The St Pancras station complex now features two additional low-level platforms, replacing Kings Cross Thameslink in offering through services from Midland Main Line suburban stations to destinations south of the Thames. These services are operated by Govia under the 'Thameslink' branding. On 29 August 2018, No. 700060 calls at the northbound platform on a service to Luton.

These Class 700 units are formed of either eight or twelve coaches, replacing the four-car Class 319 units previously operating these services. On 3 April 2017, No. 319423 calls at the low-level platforms.

As we make this journey northwards, we'll also compare today's rail scene along the line with that of the 1990s, the decade, of course, of rail privatisation. Back in 1992, the station handled UK domestic services only. On 28 June 1992, Class 56 No. 56078 stands alongside unit No. 319001 at the buffer stops. The loco survives and is currently operated by Colas Rail.

That same year saw a number of diversions of West Coast services into St Pancras as a result of the temporary closure of London Euston station. The electric locos were dragged via the Midland Main Line complete with their rakes of coaching stock. On 24 May 1992, Class 86 loco No. 86258 *Talyllyn – The First Preserved Railway* was waiting for a diesel locomotive to attach and haul it and its train northwards.

Today, the main station shares platforms with both Eurostar and Southeastern. Eurostar's London services were transferred here from Waterloo International at the end of 2007. On 5 December 2015, Eurostar's No. 373107 waits for departure on a service to Paris Gare du Nord. It will head eastwards upon leaving St Pancras and head to the Channel Tunnel via Stratford, Ebbsfleet and Ashford (Kent) using the HS1 rail lines.

Southeastern also uses this HS1 rail link to Kent. Its fleet of Class 395 'Javelin' units offers that county's travellers an alternative journey into the capital with a competitive journey time, offset somewhat by a higher ticket price. On 24 June 2014, Southeastern's Nos 395015 and 395016 are both waiting to leave on evening peak departures for the Kent coast.

By the time West Hampstead Thameslink is reached, trains from St Pancras's low-level platforms have reached ground level. This north London station has evolved into an important interchange with close-by connections to both London Overground and Jubilee line services. On 22 September 2015, No. 319444 calls on a Thameslink service.

For several years, Class 377/2 units offered a Southern livery variation. 22 September 2015 also sees No. 377209 leaving the station on the rear of a sister Class 377/5 unit, in First Capital Connect's (FCC) livery. FCC had operated services on the Midland Main Line as far north as Bedford until September 2014.

The London end of the Midland Main Line sees a few regular freight workings. One such regular working in recent years sees the loco run round its train at West Hampstead. On 11 May 2016, No. 66132 is in the process of this light engine movement. It will shortly reverse onto the northern end of the working from Cricklewood to Calvert in Buckinghamshire.

This working sees the rail transportation of containers of household waste to the site at Calvert for landfill. This rail-served waste disposal site lies a few miles south of Buckingham. On 22 September 2015, an immaculate No. 66058 *Derek Clark* pulls away from West Hampstead. The loco had recently been outshopped in the revised DB Schenker livery.

A little to the north of West Hampstead are the extensive sidings and stabling facilities at Cricklewood. A number of Thameslink's eight and twelve-car Class 700s stable here, both overnight and between daytime duties. On 27 April 2017, No. 700037 is seen stabled here from a passing Midland Main Line service.

East Midlands Trains also uses the stabling facilities here. On 5 July 2018, two of its HST power cars, Nos 43054 and 43046, are seen at the buffer stops at the north end of the yards. They are kept company by Thameslink's No. 700134.

Several commuter stations later, the Midland Main Line reaches St Albans, a distance of 17 miles from St Pancras. This popular commuting city is served by a frequent Thameslink service into the capital and beyond. Today, however, it is not served by East Midlands' longer distance services and a change of trains is required if making such journeys. On 22 September 2015, No. 319458 heads a Luton-bound service into the platform.

Until the delivery of the Class 700s, a fleet of Class 387/1 four-car units was part of the rolling stock mix, particularly on services between Bedford and Brighton. On 19 April 2016, No. 387111 leads a classmate as it approaches St Albans City station.

Luton station enjoys a frequent Thameslink service to the capital. On 22 October 2015, No. 319002 is seen arriving at the main town station. In addition, East Midlands Trains' stopping services make calls at either this station or nearby Luton Airport Parkway.

The aggregates terminal here at Luton sees regular deliveries from the quarries of Leicestershire and Derbyshire. On 8 September 2018, DB Cargo's No. 66030 waits to head north, returning its empty wagons to Peak Forest in Derbyshire.

On 2 October 2015, it's the turn of Freightliner-operated No. 66601 *The Hope Valley* to be seen shunting its wagons at the terminal. It will later return these empties to Mountsorrel in Leicestershire.

The third operator serving Luton is GB Railfreight. One of its unique liveries is carried by Class 66 loco No. 66718 *Sir Peter Hendy OBE*, seen in this photograph on 19 April 2016. On this occasion, the empty wagons will be tripped to the operator's yard at Wellingborough, in Northamptonshire, to await their next duty.

Bedford is currently the northern terminus of Thameslink services from London and the south. For the time being at least, it also remains the northernmost point of electrification on the Midland Main Line. That said, platform four has remained non-electrified and its passenger use is restricted to northbound diesel-powered services. On 14 December 2018, five-car Meridian No. 222010 calls at this platform on the 10.27 service to Corby.

It's a full house at Bedford on 1 July 2015. For a brief moment, all five lines through the station are occupied in the early afternoon. From left to right, the occupants are Nos 387117, 222018, 387120, 222013 and 222014.

Prior to their introduction on Gatwick Express services, the red-liveried Class 387/2 units brought a touch of colour to the Midland Main Line. On 16 March 2016, No. 387202 waits at Bedford prior to forming a Brighton service.

The Class 319 units were the mainstay on Thameslink services for a quarter of a century, having been delivered from the end of the 1980s onwards. By the time this photo was taken on 18 September 2015, delivery of their replacements, the Class 700 units, had already commenced. An eight-car rake, with No. 319433 nearer the camera, waits in Bedford North Siding for its next duty.

Two years later, on 10 December 2017, eight-car Class 700s were regular performers on the Bedford to Brighton service. In a wintry scene, No. 700016 waits for customers at a virtually deserted platform while No. 43047 leads a northbound HST service.

The twelve-car units are preferred on the flagship service between Bedford, Gatwick Airport and Brighton. Fewer units are required to meet Sunday service commitments, with the unit sidings at Bedford often being home to several class members. On 20 January 2019, unit Nos 700112, 700143, 700132, 700135 and 700151 are all to be seen on the stabling point.

GBRf's Class 73 locos are regularly seen along the Midland Main Line. Less common is the appearance of four of these locos in one convoy. On 11 June 2015, Nos 73961 *Alison*, 73962 *Dick Mabbutt*, 73963 *Janice* and 73964 *Jeanette* are seen heading north through Bedford on a light engine move from Tonbridge to the Brush Works at Loughborough.

The Midland Main Line sees a wide variety of diesel and electric multiple units passing through. On 4 May 2018, No. 37608 *Andromeda* heads south through Bedford, dragging Crossrail unit No. 345019 on a move from the test track at Old Dalby, near Melton Mowbray in Leicestershire, to Wembley.

A variety of charter trains can also be seen on the Midland Main Line, with Chatsworth House, near Chesterfield in Derbyshire, a frequent destination for passengers. On 7 June 2017, No. 67015 heads north from Bedford with one such working from London Victoria to Chesterfield. DB Cargo's Class 66 No. 66013 is on the rear of the train.

Class 67s also make regular appearances during the leaf fall season, working Rail Head Treatment Trains (RHTTs) in top'n'tail mode. Colas Rail's pair of Class 67s, Nos 67023 *Stella* and 67027 *Charlotte*, were heading south through Bedford on these RHTT duties on 16 November 2018. The pair's diagram commenced at Toton depot, on the county boundaries of Derbyshire and Nottinghamshire. They will reverse at West Hampstead before returning north.

Bedford's main station (formerly Midland Road) became the terminus of the 16-mile branch from Bletchley, via a short spur from nearby St John's station. This followed the closure of the remainder of the Varsity Line between Oxford and Cambridge in 1967. A long overdue reopening of the full line looks increasingly likely, under the East West Rail Consortium. On 30 October 2017, London Northwestern Railway's No. 153334 stands in Bedford's bay platform, waiting to form the 09.29 to Bletchley.

These services are operated by London Northwestern Railway's units, based at its depot at Tyseley, south of Birmingham. One Class 150 and one Class 153 are the usual traction, outstabling at Bletchley. On 16 July 2016, No. 150105 has just terminated at Bedford on a mid-afternoon service from Bletchley.

On 7 December 2016, single-car Class 153 unit No. 153375 waits in the same bay platform, ready to form the 09.29 to Bletchley.

In 1999, the then operator, Silverlink, used a pair of Fragonset-operated Class 31s to operate Marston Vale services until the availability of its own units improved. On 28 July that year, No. 31452 is seen at the buffer stop in Bedford's bay platform. Sister loco No. 31602 will lead the two-coach train when it departs for Bletchley.

In another look back to Network South East days, Bedford electric multiple unit stabling point is home to three Class 319 units on 21 April 1991. These NSE units are Nos 319179 (which was renumbered to 319379), 319164 (which became No. 319364) and 319008.

The 1990s also saw regular loco stabling at Bedford. On the same day in 1991, Nos 56070 and 31112 were to be found stabled here.

They were in the company of a pair of Class 20s owned by Hunslet-Barclay, used on weedkiller trains. With a sister loco out of view, No. 20902 is stabled with its train over the weekend.

At a quick glance, this shot could have been taken around the same time. In fact, it was taken on 12 February 2019. A pair of Class 20s, Nos 20189 (in blue) and 20142 (in London Transport livery), are approaching Bedford station on a light engine move from Derby to Bletchley. The pair, on a Loram Rail working, were to collect a track machine from the former depot there.

Another important aggregate flow sees regular deliveries from Mountsorrel to Elstow, on the southern outskirts of Bedford. On 3 July 2018, No. 66003 passes Oakley, to the north of Bedford, with a loaded working.

The same overbridge at Oakley is the location for this view, this time looking south. DB Schenker was the operator of the stone traffic from Peak Forest to Bletchley back in 2017. On 30 September that year, No. 66135 had failed at the terminal, requiring assistance in order to return the empties north. No. 60066 was called upon to assist, offering a rare chance to witness one of that company's dwindling Class 60 fleet on this stretch of the Midland Main Line.

Direct Rail Services' Class 66 locomotives are also rarely seen in the area. On 19 February 2018, No. 66422 approaches Oakley on a returning engineers' working from Kettering North Junction to Whitemoor Yard, near March in Cambridgeshire. It is heading south in order to run round its train at Bedford before heading back north.

Preliminary work in connection with electrification of the line north of Bedford is currently underway. By 2 February 2019, erection of the masts has commenced as Colas Rail's No. 37521 heads north past Oakley on a Dollands Moor to Derby returning Network Rail test train. The station here closed to passengers in 1958.

The next station north of Bedford is Wellingborough, with a distance of 15 miles between the two. It currently enjoys a twice-hourly passenger service south to St Pancras, with hourly northbound services to both Nottingham and Corby. On 3 August 2018, No. 222103 calls at Wellingborough on a Corby to London service.

Locos operated by the Rail Operations Group are frequent users of the Midland Main Line. On 3 August 2018, Class 37 loco No. 37800 *Cassiopeia* is seen heading north through the station, returning light engine from Wembley to Leicester.

For many years, the delivery of aviation fuel from Lindsey, on south Humberside, to Colnbrook (for Heathrow Airport) brought tank trains to the Midland Main Line. Operated by Colas Rail in recent years, its Class 60 loco, No. 60056, heads north through Wellingborough on the return working of the empty tanks on 15 April 2015.

Freightliner's Class 66/6 locos are also regular performers on the Midland Main Line. On 15 April 2016, No. 66605 approaches Wellingborough station on a working from Earles Sidings, near Hope in Derbyshire, to West Thurrock in Essex.

Direct Rail Services' Class 37 locos have been regular visitors to the Midland Main Line in recent years. In particular these locomotives are found on Network Rail Test Trains, operating to and from their Derby base. On 28 March 2014, No. 37610 is seen approaching Wellingborough.

It is partnered by No. 37425 *Sir Robert McAlpine/Concrete Bob* on the rear. The pair are destined for a few days on the former Southern Region, initially working from Derby to Hither Green, in south-east London. Freightliner's No. 66615 can be seen passing through the station, heading north.

To the north of Wellingborough station is the yard now used as a base by GBRf for wagon moves in this area of the Midland Main Line. On 17 April 2016, the yard is occupied by No. 66718 *Sir Peter Hendy OBE* along with an assortment of GBRf wagons.

A little further to the north of Wellingborough lies Harrowden Junction. This vantage point is popular among local photographers, although erection of the electrification masts is now underway, together with reinstatement of the four-track railway between Wellingborough and Kettering. On 2 November 2017, HST power car No. 43064 leads a southbound working from Nottingham to St Pancras.

GBRf now handles much of the freight traffic on this section of the MML, including the stone workings to and from the Leicestershire quarry at Bardon Hill. On 2 November 2017, No. 66769 heads north past the junction with a return working of empty hoppers from Colnbrook, near Heathrow, to Bardon Hill.

GBRf also handles the traffic to and from the cement works at Ketton, near Stamford in Lincolnshire. This working operates several days a week to the terminal just to the north of St Pancras. At the time of this photo, taken on 27 February 2018, the operation was in the hands of DB Cargo. Its Class 66 loco, No. 66030, heads the empties northwards. The train will leave the MML at Syston, north of Leicester, and head east towards to its destination.

Kettering station, 65 miles from St Pancras, serves Northamptonshire's second largest town (behind Northampton itself) as well as being the MML junction for the nearby town of Corby. On 13 December 2018, an East Midlands Trains HST is substituting for a booked five-car Meridian unit on the 09.53 departure to Corby. Power car No. 43058 is on the rear, nearer the camera, with No. 43047 leading.

Six HST power cars were transferred to East Midlands Trains from East Coast Main Line operator Grand Central by Arriva at the beginning of 2018. A pair of these are regular performers on Kettering's 17.46 departure to Corby. On 6 February 2019, No. 43465 awaits departure time on the rear of this service.

The town of Corby is reached by a 7-mile spur from the Midland Main Line north of Kettering. On 20 May 2016, five-car Meridian No. 222022 stands in the single platform, waiting to return to London. This photo was taken before the reinstatement of double track and erection of electrification masts.

The annual autumn 'leaf fall' Rail Head Treatment Trains were operated in 2018 by Colas Rail. This working included the lines from Toton southwards to West Hampstead, for reversal. For most of the season, Colas's own pair of Class 67s were used, as seen through Bedford earlier in this publication. Alternative duties for these locomotives on 26 November 2018 saw a rare appearance of Class 70s that day, with No. 70812 leading No. 70809, approaching Kettering station from the north.

On 21 December 2012, GBRf's No. 66735 makes a brief stop in Kettering station. It was in the process of moving Nos 66747, 66748 *West Burton 50* and 66749, which had recently been purchased by the UK operator. Following a period in storage in the Netherlands, the three newly acquired locos were moved to the Midland Railway Centre at Butterley, in Derbyshire, as a light engine convoy from Dollands Moor.

Great Western Railway 'Hall' Class 4-6-0 steam loco No. 4965 *Rood Ashton Hall* waits at Kettering on 25 August 2003. It worked several trips between here and Melton Mowbray, crossing Harringworth Viaduct in the process. The trains were run to celebrate the 125th anniversary of the viaduct's opening.

On the morning of 30 January 2017, a Monday, a pair of GBRf Class 66s, Nos 66768 and 66727 *Maritime One*, wait in Kettering station while working a returning engineers' train to Toton. They had spent the weekend employed on infrastructure work at Harrow on the Hill in north-west London.

Around twenty years earlier, on 18 February 1996, a Sunday, No. 58047 *Manton Colliery*, which had recently become an EWS loco under privatisation, waits in almost the same spot. It is also about to return to Toton, this time from an engineers' possession further south on the Midland Main Line.

The modified electrification plan extends only as far as Kettering North Junction on the MML and then onwards to Corby. The next station northward, Market Harborough, will remain non-electrified although significant track realignment is scheduled to 'straighten' the tight curves here. On 13 October 2015, Freightliner's No. 66620 takes the curve north through the station on a return working of empty cement tanks from Theale, near Reading, to Earles Sidings in Derbyshire's Hope Valley.

Sister Freightliner loco No. 66953 is seen heading in the opposite direction through Market Harborough platforms on 13 October 2016. It is in the process of delivering electric multiple unit No. 387303 from Derby to Bletchley depot.

Another Network Rail working through Market Harborough on 13 October 2015 sees its own Class 73, No. 73138, paired with GBRf's No. 73212 *Fiona* (on the rear) as they return their train from Tonbridge, in Kent, to the test train base at Derby.

Prior to delivery of its Class 222 fleet of Meridians, East Midlands Trains stopping services to and from St Pancras were in the hands of Class 170 diesel units. Sporting the much-loved 'teal and tangerine' livery formerly used on the company's fleet, three-car unit No. 170106 calls on a service towards St Pancras. The photo was taken around the time of the millennium.

Knighton Junction, to the south of Leicester station, sees the diverging branch towards Coalville and Burton-on-Trent. Reinstatement of the passenger service between Leicester and these towns remains a distant pipedream. The line is, however, used for regular freight traffic, particularly to Bardon Hill. The sidings have been used to offload locomotives delivered to Leicester by road. For example, on 22 June 2018, Class 27 loco No. 27059 waits to be moved.

On 14 December 2018, it's the turn of Class 37 loco No. 37207, waiting to be moved to the nearby depot at Leicester. It had just arrived by low-loader from Barrow Hill, in Derbyshire. It has a rail grinder for company, with the Burton branch heading off to the left of the photo.

Leicester station is an important interchange for East Midlands Trains' customers switching from services to and from Sheffield, via Derby, and Nottingham. On 11 July 2014, No. 222102 has just arrived at the London-bound platform and will now run non-stop to St Pancras.

Services were severely disrupted on 23 February 2017, with the culprit being Storm 'Doris'. With the station deserted at around 20.00 hours, the author was relieved to head home with power car No. 43081 arriving on an additional stopping service for the south.

The Midland Main Line has a long association with the HST. On 4 May 1994, InterCity-liveried power car No. 43055 *The Sheffield Star 125 Years* is seen on the rear of a service leaving Leicester for St Pancras.

By 19 May 1998, 'Midland Mainline' branding had been applied to the fleet. Sister power car No. 43056 is also seen on the rear of a St Pancras-bound service.

Leicester station is also an important crossroads for services operating north to south by East Midlands Trains and east to west services by Arriva-owned CrossCountry Trains (XC). These XC services are formed of two and three-car Class 170 diesel units. They operate twice-hourly west to Birmingham New Street and hourly eastwards to Stansted Airport via Peterborough and Cambridge. On 23 October 2017, two-car unit No. 170117 is awaiting departure on the 16.18 to Stansted Airport.

The service pattern at Leicester is completed by an hourly stopping service to Lincoln, via Nottingham. On 25 March 2015, No. 156408 arrives at Leicester on a terminating service from Lincoln.

On 13 March 2017, single-carriage Class 153 unit No. 153313 is arriving on a similar working. This busy scene looking north from the station platform also shows No. 66030 running round its wagons in the sidings at Humberstone Road. In the distance, seven-car Meridian No. 222002 *The Cutlers' Company* waits at the signals for the 153 unit to clear the section.

On Mondays and Fridays these local Leicester to Lincoln services include a diagram for one of EMT's four-car Meridian units. On 14 December 2018, No. 222101 arrives at Leicester.

The regular pattern of passenger services is broken by the occasional movement of other operators' stock for works attention. On 6 December 2017, South Western Railway's Class 158 unit No. 158890 heads south sporting its new corporate livery. It is returning from Brush's workshops at Loughborough to its home depot at Salisbury.

Equally unusual was this move on 15 February 2012. First Great Western's Adelante unit No. 180106 passed through Leicester on a move from its home depot of Old Oak Common, in west London, to Brodie's workshops at Kilmarnock, in Scotland.

Leicester station sees regular appearances of Direct Rail Services (DRS) locos on ballast workings from both Crewe and Carlisle to the quarry at Mountsorrel, a few miles to the north. On 8 January 2019, No. 66426 is DRS's chosen traction for the morning working from Crewe to Mountsorrel.

Monday morning sees GBRf positioning its locos for the workings in the week ahead. This includes a light engine convoy, often including wagons returning from exam or repair, from its Peterborough depot to the container terminal at Hams Hall, West Midlands. On 7 January 2019, No. 66723 *Chinook* brings up the rear of a five-loco move with Nos 66705 *Golden Jubilee*, 66727 *Maritime One*, 66774 and 66719 *Metro-Land* at the front of the convoy.

Class 60 locos have a long association with the Leicester area. On 28 March 2018, Colas Rail's No. 60056 heads north on the goods loop on the return empty aviation fuel tanks from Colnbrook to Lindsey.

The remaining DB Cargo examples of the class have been less common in recent years. On 5 March 2015, No. 60063, then a DB Cargo loco, is stabled adjacent to the former depot with a rake of empty Lafarge wagons.

In the 1990s it was common practice for the 100 members of the class to carry the livery of the Railfreight sector for which they operated. Sporting its construction livery, No. 60094 *Tryfan* is working light engine on to Leicester depot on 28 September 1993.

Rail privatisation in the mid-1990s brought many changes to the Railfreight sector, with the Class 60 fleet operated by the English, Welsh & Scottish Railway quickly falling out of favour. The Class 66 was heralded as the much-needed modern replacement. During this period of change, No. 60055 *Thomas Barnado* comes off the depot, with a pair of Class 58 locos visible in the distance, on 1 May 1998. It carried the TransRail branding at the time.

The widespread use of Class 08 diesel shunters on the UK rail network is now but a distant memory. On 4 August 1992, locally based No. 08697 awaits its next duty.

At the time, much of the Royal Mail's business was handled by the rail industry, with many locos carrying the dedicated livery of Rail Express Systems. This photo, also taken on 4 August 1992, sees Class 47 Brush Type 4 loco No. 47631 arriving at Leicester at the head of Royal Mail vans.

On 2 September 1994, a pair of Railfreight-liveried Class 31s, with No. 31149 leading No. 31247, are seen passing the depot at Leicester on a southbound infrastructure working.

The Redland stone self-discharge trains were still in use until a few years ago. This view, taken on 14 May 1998, shows Class 58 loco No. 58048 in charge as it passes the depot, displaying its maroon and gold EWS branding.

In 2013, the depot at Leicester, which had long been unused by DB Schenker, was returned to use by UK Rail Leasing. Since then, a wide range of loco classes have been on view there, resembling the old-style diesel depots in their heyday. This view on 14 December 2018 shows, from left to right, Nos 37608 *Andromeda*, 50008 *Thunderer*, 56091, 37503, 56060 and 33053 in the depot yard.

For several years, No. 37670 was a particular favourite in the depot. Now consigned to history, the distinctively repainted DB Cargo loco is visible from the station platform end in this view of the depot complex on 13 March 2017.

A brighter future surely awaits another Class 37 loco favourite. Looking resplendent in its newly applied Europhoenix colours, No. 37901 *Mirrlees Pioneer* was in full view on the main line side of the depot complex on 11 January 2019.

Virgin Trains' livery is rarely seen on the Midland Main Line. On 8 September 2011, however, a trio of Class 57 locomotives, Nos 57305, 57303 and 57301, paused in Leicester station platform on a northbound light engine move.

The local stations between Leicester and Loughborough were re-opened in 1993 and marketed as the Ivanhoe line. On 12 April 2018, East Midlands Trains Class 156 unit No. 156470 slows to call at Sileby on a Leicester service.

On the same day, seven-car Meridian unit No. 222006 *The Carbon Cutter* passes Sileby on a London St Pancras to Sheffield express service.

Shortly after the Meridian had passed, Sileby saw two Class 66s pass through within a couple of minutes of each other. First, GBRf's No. 66782 passes through on a Whitemoor Yard to Toton light engine working.

Then, it's the turn of a DB Cargo Class 66 to head south through Sileby. The sight of a DB Cargo loco with a rake of 'HTA' coal hoppers was once a familiar one. Today, such workings are much less common. Here, No. 66138 is at the head of an additional working from Scunthorpe to Margam Yard, in South Wales.

The rail-served Leicestershire quarry at Mountsorrel sees a number of trainloads of aggregates leave here for a variety of destinations. On 21 July 2016, GBRf's Class 66 No. 66720 is waiting in the quarry sidings before taking its trainload back to Whitemoor Yard.

The headshunt at the north end of the Mountsorrel complex is the location in this photo on 4 July 2016. DRS's No. 68020 *Reliance* is likewise waiting to pick up its wagons and return to Crewe Basford Hall yard.

This working from Crewe arrives at Mountsorrel from the south having run via Nuneaton and Leicester. The return loaded working leaves the quarry sidings by heading north through Loughborough, where No. 68001 *Evolution* is seen on 27 May 2016.

A few years earlier, Freightliner operated this particular working, often utilising one of its Class 70 locos. On 1 May 2013, the return working passes Loughborough with No. 70015 in charge. It will reach the West Coast Main Line at Lichfield via the short freight-only branch from Burton-on-Trent.

The seven-car Meridians on EMT's flagship Sheffield to London services do not routinely call at Loughborough. On 21 March 2017, No. 222003 *Tornado* passes through, heading south to London. The spur into the Brush workshops can be seen veering off to the right, above the train.

The third platform at Loughborough is served by the local Ivanhoe services in both directions. On 26 April 2018, No. 158889, itself once operated by sister company South West Trains, is about to call while heading north on a Lincoln service.

The Brush workshops handle a variety of work for the various train operating companies. On 24 March 2015, West Coast Railway Company's Class 37 loco No. 37706 is about to head into the works while delivering a Chiltern Railways driving vehicle trailer, No. 82102.

On 1 September 2014, a GBRf loco convoy arrives at Loughborough. Class 66 loco No. 66728 is delivering Nos 73005 and 73006 to the workshops. They would emerge renumbered as 73966 and 73967 respectively.

Several local footpaths offer perimeter views into the Brush works yard at Loughborough. On 24 September 2016, Chiltern Railways two-car unit No. 168323 awaits its release from the works.

On 28 January 2017, a pair of Class 92 locos, Nos 92006 *Louis Armand* and 92020 *Milton*, can be seen in this view across the field.

As mentioned earlier, East Midlands Trains acquired several power cars from Grand Central at the beginning of 2018. Just ahead of entering service with EMT, power car No. 43468 leads a rake of empty stock on a proving run on 13 April that year. It is approaching Loughborough station platform on a circular outing from Derby Etches Park depot.

On 10 October 2014, No. 66152 *Derek Holmes Railway Operator* heads south through Loughborough on a load of steel coils from Margam Yard, in South Wales, to Corby.

The station at East Midlands Parkway, 104 miles from St Pancras, was opened in 2009, primarily to serve the nearby airport. On 1 February 2019, five-car Meridian No. 222010 calls on a London-bound service. The station is dwarfed by the cooling towers of the adjacent power station at Ratcliffe-on-Soar.

The same day sees GBRf's No. 66728 *Institute of Railway Operators* heading north through the station. It is taking a rake of empty wagons from the company's Wellingborough Yard to Rylstone, near Skipton in North Yorkshire, for loading.

Just to the north of East Midlands Parkway lies Trent Junction. The station closed in 1968, but the triangle here sees the lines to Derby and Nottingham diverge, together with a more direct line that heads north along the Erewash Valley, passing Toton Yard. Immediately after the junction on the westerly fork towards Derby lies Long Eaton station. On 1 February 2019, CrossCountry unit No. 170116 calls on a service from Nottingham to Birmingham via Derby.

The Derby to Nottingham corridor sees a frequent service between the two cities. In addition to the twice-hourly CrossCountry Services, East Midlands Trains links the two with a through service from Matlock to Newark Castle. On the same day, single-car units Nos 153311 and 153374 approach Long Eaton on a Newark service.

The city of Derby, 111 miles from St Pancras, has a long and proud link to both building and maintaining Britain's railway locomotives, dating back to the mid-nineteenth century. On nationalisation of our railways in 1947, the vast complex became part of BR Workshops. Today, the work continues with private companies still building multiple units in the area. On 18 March 2018, two Class 710 vehicles are seen outside Bombardier Transportation's Litchurch Lane complex. These electric units are destined for London Overground.

London Underground (LUL) is another important customer of Bombardier Transportation in Derby. GBRf is contracted to move its units between Derby, the test track at Old Dalby and LUL's depot at West Ruislip in London. On 21 September 2017, four Class 20 locos, Nos 20314, 20311, 20107 and 20905, are seen waiting alongside Derby station. They will shortly enter the works yard to collect a LUL unit for delivery to Old Dalby.

Derby is also an important interchange for passengers, with cross-country services from the North East to the South West sharing the Midland Main Line between here and Sheffield. On 5 December 2017, CrossCountry five-car Voyager No. 221141 arrives at Derby, forming the 10.44 service to Edinburgh Waverley.

CrossCountry also has a small fleet of High Speed Train sets that supplement its frequent Voyager services. On 8 March 2018, No. 43207 leads a rake of HST coaches with power car No. 43378 on the rear. They are arriving on a service bound for Plymouth.

East Midlands Trains operates an hourly service between Derby and Crewe usually formed of single-car Class 153 diesel units. On 8 March 2018, No. 153313 waits to form the 10.42 service to Crewe.

The Railway Technical Centre (RTC) on London Road in Derby dates back to the 1960s in the days of the British Railways Board. Today, the locos and rolling stock for Network Rail's test trains are based here. This view shows the line-up on 31 March 2017. From right to left, the locos are Nos 37608, 37025 *Inverness TMD Quality Assured*, 31459, 31233, 08645, 08762, 73101, 73139, a Class 45 carrying no number (No. 45118) and No. 31105.

This is a typically busy scene at the RTC, glimpsed in passing on the Midland Main Line on 6 September 2016. Gathered outside the workshops are Nos 73951 *Malcolm Brinded*, 37038, 37558 *Avro Vulcan XH558* (No. 37424 in reality), 37194, 97303 and 68005 *Defiant*.

The Derby area enjoys as wide a diversity of traction types as just about anywhere in the country. This photograph, taken on 26 October 2017, shows Nos 50008 *Thunderer* and 31452 stabled alongside the station platform.

On 8 September 2016, this trio of locos were parked up in almost the same place. Class 46 No. 46045, carrying the number D182, is in the company of Nos 20059 and 20188. The Class 44, 45 and 46 'Peak' locomotives have been synonymous with Derby for over half a century.

An exceptionally rare move through Derby on 13 October 2014 also involved the pair of Class 20s featured earlier, namely Nos 20311 and 20314. They were called upon to collect No. 59003 from the docks at Immingham, south Humberside, and take it to Eastleigh Works for attention. The former Foster Yeoman Class 59 had spent the previous seventeen years in Germany. The author was delighted to see it still carrying its *Yeoman Highlander* nameplates.

Another pair of Class 20s are seen stabled at Derby on 14 June 2014. Then privately owned, Nos 20142 and 20189 briefly sported the striking colours of Balfour Beatty.

Derby sees regular Direct Rail Services loco convoys between here and the company's depot at Crewe Gresty Bridge. Half a century separates the ages of these pairs of locos seen arriving on 21 July 2016. Class 37s Nos 37606 and 37612 were delivered new to British Railways in 1963. Making up the quartet are Class 68 locos Nos 68005 *Defiant* and 68022 *Resolution*. These two were built in 2014 at Vossloh's base in Valencia, Spain.

Most freight traffic in the area is booked via Toton and the Erewash Valley, thereby avoiding Derby station. One regular working that is routed via Derby station is seen on 6 June 2018. By then in the hands of GBRf, its Class 66 loco No. 66747 heads north with empty hoppers from Washwood Heath, in Birmingham, returning to Peak Forest in Derbyshire.

Since railway privatisation in 1994, this traffic had previously been handled by DB Cargo. This photo is taken at the time of our railways' transition into private ownership. On 30 July that year, Class 60 loco No. 60016 *Langdale Pikes* heads south through Derby on the loaded working towards Birmingham.

In 2001, the same company also handled the contract for movement of Royal Mail vans around the UK, with Derby being an important mail hub. The Class 67 locos were originally ordered to handle this postal traffic. On 8 May that year, No. 67022 waits for its vans to be loaded in Derby's platform before heading south.

Another short-lived livery is seen in this view of Class 37 No. 37688 at Derby on a light engine move on 17 October 1997. Loadhaul was one of the businesses, and therefore brands, created around the time of privatisation and the early evolution of the business that was to become DB Cargo. The loco had lost its *Coedbach* nameplates by this date and was cut up at Booths in Rotherham in early 2010.

As already mentioned, the line between Derby and Manchester was highlighted by the Beeching Report to be an unneeded duplicate route between London and Manchester. As a result, the section between Matlock and Buxton was inexplicably closed by the Minister for Transport as a through passenger route in 1968. At the southern end of this line, the section between Derby and Matlock was retained, with a single-track branch line leaving the Midland Main Line at Ambergate Junction. On 22 March 2018, a pair of Class 153 units, Nos 153311 and 153313, call at Duffield on a Matlock service.

Longer distance passengers between Derby and Manchester were left with little choice but to travel via Sheffield, with a change of trains there. Duffield is again the location on 22 March 2018 as a pair of Class 222 Meridians, with No. 222014 leading, head south on a Sheffield to St Pancras service.

In our journey northwards on the Midland Main Line, it's time to backtrack to Trent Junction, where the Erewash Valley line bisects the cities of Derby and Nottingham. Shortly after the junction, No. 60079 is seen passing close to Long Eaton town centre on 21 May 2013. By that date, DB Cargo Class 60-hauled coal trains had become a rarity. This empty hopper working was heading from Ratcliffe power station to Warrington's Arpley Yard. The loco had just run round its train in nearby Toton Yard.

There are limited booked passenger services through the Toton Yard area, although it is regularly used as a diversionary route, often planned and sometimes in an emergency. On 28 January 2017, East Midlands Trains Class 158 No. 158777 passes through the yard.

DB Cargo, one of the freight businesses that has evolved since rail privatisation, has a twenty-year-long association with Toton, its major operations hub. It has changed hands and corporate branding since its unveiling as English, Welsh & Scottish Railways in the mid-1990s. Its assets included the fleet of 100 Class 60 locos. Today, the majority of this fleet is out of traffic, with others sold to competitors. In a typical view from the nearby bank, taken on 28 January 2017, No. 60067 leads a line of stored Class 60s.

The fleet of thirty Class 67 locos also passed into DB Cargo's hands on privatisation. Since the railway's loss of Royal Mail traffic, they have seen limited use. On 24 September 2016, No. 67029 *Royal Diamond* is stabled in the Toton depot area.

The depot open day on 29 August 1998 gave many enthusiasts their first glimpse of a Class 66 locomotive. Recently delivered No. 66004 was one of several early examples on display that day. A total fleet of 250 was to be delivered to DB Cargo (then EWS), although the fleet has since been reduced by about half with transfers to Europe and sales to other UK operators.

Almost twenty years later, on 19 April 2017, No. 66017 is in the foreground of this typical view of a number of Class 66s stabled on the north end of the depot.

Colas Rail's small fleet of Class 66s are regular visitors to the depot for servicing purposes. On 14 April 2016, one of them, No. 66847, stands at the depot.

Other operators visit the extensive yards in the Toton area, chiefly on infrastructure workings. On 19 April 2017, Direct Rail Services Class 66 No. 66426 has just arrived in the yard.

In this view of the yard on 12 June 2018, it's the turn of Freightliner-operated No. 66547 to be seen on an engineers' working. It had just arrived from a weekend engineering possession on the southern end of the Midland Main Line.

The New Year weekend of 2017/18 was an ideal opportunity for extensive engineering activity, with a number of trains booked out of Toton by various operators, including GBRf. Its Class 66 No. 66766 waits at the head of its train on 1 January 2018. Several long term stored Class 60s are visible in the depot's training compound beyond.

It's time to backtrack to Trent Junction and this time take the eastern fork towards Nottingham. The station at Beeston has become increasingly popular for customers on the western edge of the city of Nottingham. On 10 October 2014, EMT's No. 156411 calls on a local service from Leicester to Lincoln Central.

Another Lincoln-bound service calls at Beeston on 1 March 2016. This time it is formed of two-car Class 158 No. 158810.

To the east of Beeston station lies an important Network Rail infrastructure yard. DB Cargo Class 66s handle regular trip workings between here and Toton Yard. On 19 April 2017, No. 66155 is seen shunting its train in readiness to return to Toton.

The yard also sees regular trips to and from Doncaster, handled by DRS Class 66s. On 24 April 2017, No. 66432 is marshalling its trainload for return to Doncaster.

Nottingham is the terminus for most services arriving in the city from London St Pancras, 107 miles away. A few peak hour services continue northwards to Sheffield and Leeds. This involves reversal in the station. On 14 April 2016, No. 222101 has just terminated and is being prepared for its return to St Pancras. CrossCountry unit No. 170111 can be seen on the left. It, too, has just terminated, having arrived on a service from Birmingham New Street.

As already mentioned, services in the Derby to Nottingham corridor include an hourly through service from Newark Castle to Matlock. On 26 June 2018, No. 156415 leaves Nottingham for Derby and Matlock.

Stations between Nottingham and Chesterfield are shared between East Midlands Trains and Northern by Arriva. The latter company operates an hourly stopping service linking Nottingham and Sheffield, and northwards to Leeds. On 6 February 2019, Northern's two-car Class 158 unit No. 158817 has just terminated at Nottingham and is preparing to work the 11.15 to Leeds.

The procession of diesel units at Nottingham is occasionally interrupted by a loco appearance. Network Rail Test Trains often produce a pair of Class 37 locos, as was the case on 11 May 2018. Colas Rail's No. 37116 leads a circular working from Derby to Skegness and return.

The East Midlands has seen a dramatic downturn in coal traffic in recent years. The power station at nearby Ratcliffe-on-Soar is, however, still served by a number of workings each week from the port of Immingham. DB Cargo's No. 66120 passes through Nottingham station on a loaded working to the power station on 22 March 2013.

On 17 June 2015, it's the turn of Freightliner's No. 66520 to head west through Nottingham on a similar loaded working from Humberside.

On 6 February 2019, GBRf's No. 66751 *Inspiration Delivered Hitachi Rail Europe* has just received the signal to proceed in the opposite direction, taking the line towards Lincoln on a rake of empty hoppers from Ratcliffe to Immingham.

The days of Nottingham station requiring a shunting loco have long gone. In this view on 5 May 1990, No. 08511 stands in the bay platform at the east end of the station, awaiting its next duty. This platform is now primarily used for Skegness-bound services.

Several stations between Nottingham and Chesterfield have been reopened since closure under the Beeching Axe in the 1960s. Most recently, Ilkeston station was reopened in April 2017. On 22 June 2018, Northern's No. 150271 calls on a Nottingham to Leeds service.

Ilkeston station sees a number of rail movements into and out of Toton Yard from the north. On 22 June 2018, a pair of DB Cargo's Class 66 locomotives, Nos 66151 and 66174, are passing south on a light engine move from Doncaster to Toton.

A little further north, Alfreton & Mansfield Parkway station was opened in 1973 as one of the first park'n'ride concept stations in the UK. Mansfield has since regained its own passenger service, with the Parkway station reverting to the name Alfreton. On 13 April 2018, No. 158901 calls on a Nottingham to Leeds service.

A few minutes later that day, GBRf's No. 66745 *Modern Railways The First 50 Years* passes through the same platform at Alfreton on a light engine move. It has taken a particularly circuitous route from Peterborough to Doncaster.

The lines from Derby and Nottingham converge just south of Chesterfield. On 19 July 2016, Northern's No. 150276 calls on a service from Leeds which will take the Nottingham fork a couple of miles south of the station.

On 21 September 2017, Midland Main Line's Meridian No. 222009 stands in the southbound platform on a service for London St Pancras. Meanwhile, competitor CrossCountry's Voyager No. 221132 has just arrived at the northbound platform on a service from Penzance to Glasgow Central.

Northern has taken delivery of a number of Class 170 units previously in use with ScotRail. On 11 April 2018, No. 170475 passes through Chesterfield's southbound platform on an empty stock working from Leeds Holbeck to Nottingham. By this date, the unit's ScotRail branding had been removed.

Chesterfield station enjoys a diverse range of light engine moves. On 19 April 2017, GBRf's Caledonian Sleeper loco No. 73971 is seen heading south on a working from Edinburgh's Craigentinny depot to the Brush workshops at Loughborough.

A year earlier, on 5 July 2016, Deltic No. 55009 *Alycidon* and Class 40 loco No. 40013 are seen heading south, taking a circuitous route on a light engine move from Grosmont, on the North Yorkshire Moors Railway, to Crewe.

The Midland Main Line sees relatively few container trains throughout its length. This northern section does, however, see Freightliner services to and from the terminal at Stourton, near Leeds. On 13 April 2018, No. 66519, with sister loco No. 66524 for company, heads south through Chesterfield on a service from Leeds to Southampton.

Colas Rail's Class 70 locos are occasional visitors to the area. On 8 June 2017, No. 70814 heads south on a working from Stourton to Briton Ferry yard in South Wales.

The many collieries in the Chesterfield area ensured that the station saw a regular flow of 'merry-go-round' coal wagons. In a typical scene, No. 56087 heads south with a loaded coal working on 4 August 1992. The loco survives in traffic and is in service with Colas Rail.

The north Derbyshire station at Dronfield had closed at the end of 1966. It was to be reopened in 1981 with a limited service during peak hours only. It is now being served primarily by the Northern by Arriva hourly service between Nottingham and Leeds. On 6 February 2019, No. 158817 calls on a Leeds-bound service.

The same day, EMT's Meridian No. 222021 heads south through Dronfield. It is seen passing the old British Railways-style station name sign, the colour denoting the former Eastern Region.

The Hope Valley line joins the Midland Main Line at Dore & Totley, on the southern outskirts of Sheffield. Local services on the Hope Valley have been regularly worked by Class 142 Pacer units since their introduction in the mid-1980s. Back on 27 April 1996, No. 142084 calls at Dore & Totley on its way to Sheffield.

These services use a dedicated south-facing bay platform at Sheffield. On 13 October 2016, No. 142055 waits in the bay to return to Manchester via all stations along the Hope Valley.

Sheffield station is the northern terminus of the twice-hourly services from London St Pancras. On 3 September 2015, No. 222021 has just terminated and is being prepared for its return journey to London. The fastest workings cover the distance of 140 miles between this Yorkshire city and the capital in just under two hours.

Several passenger service operators serve Sheffield, including CrossCountry Trains, using the 32-mile stretch of the Midland Main Line between Derby and Sheffield. On 22 February 2017, No. 221127 calls on a service to Edinburgh Waverley.

First TransPennine Express shares the Midland Main Line, albeit briefly, with its east to west service between Cleethorpes and Manchester Airport. On 18 May 2017, No. 185147 calls at Sheffield on a service for Manchester Airport.

Northern Class 150s are now regular performers on the stopping services to and from Sheffield to Manchester Piccadilly. On 9 March 2016, No. 150137 terminates on a service from Manchester.

East Midlands Trains services between Norwich and Liverpool Lime Street reverse in the platform at Sheffield, with a pair of units, usually Class 158s, working on the section west of Nottingham. On the evening of 10 December 2015, Class 156 unit No. 156408 is paired with a Class 158 unit as they wait to leave Sheffield via the Hope Valley line to Manchester and Liverpool.

Reflecting Sheffield's long association with the High Speed Train, No. 43196 calls at the station in 1995. The InterCity-liveried power car leads a service to Swansea.

The short section of the Midland Main Line between Sheffield and Dore & Totley sees regular services to Earles Sidings on the Hope Valley line. On 19 September 2013, No. 70003 is paired with No. 66618 *Railways Illustrated Annual Photographic Awards – Alan Barnes*, heading north through Sheffield on a light engine move from Earles to Freightliner's depot in Leeds.

Workings out of these sidings and the nearby Hope Cement Works have been an important revenue source for our railways for many decades. On 5 August 1992, in the days before privatisation, Class 37 loco No. 37687 heads a rake of cement empties through Sheffield, returning to Earles Sidings.

In the 1990s, our railways were still handling a sizeable amount of Royal Mail business. On 3 August 1993, No. 47599 is waiting in Sheffield to back onto a rake of General Utility Vans.

The Tinsley Depot open day on 27 April 1996 saw several tours that terminated at Sheffield. Bearing a 'Current Thinking' headboard, National Power's Class 59 loco No. 59205 is seen with a classmate as they await their next move.